To.....

From....

D1471459

First published 2002 by Contender Books
Contender Books is a division of
The Contender Entertainment Group
48 Margaret Street
London W1W 8SE

3 5 7 9 10 8 6 4 2

ISBN 1-84357-027-0

Printed in Italy

CHRISTMAS HUGS

Having you here makes a lovely time
Absolutely perfect.

Let's make this Christmas
One that we'll always remember.

I can't think of anyone
I'd rather spend Christmas day with than you.

If my Christmas wish comes true,
I'll soon be hugging you.

Let's make this
the most lovable Christmas ever.

I simply want to say,
Have a very special day.

Something sweet to help us celebrate
This very happy time.

Christmas is the time
For parties, laughter
And hugging you.

I can't be with you this Christmas day.
But I'm sending hugs from far away.

That was the nicest Christmas
I can remember.
Can I thank you with a hug?

I want to wish you the happiest Christmas
From the bottom of my heart.

Being with you is the best present of all.

I wish you could be here for Christmas...

... and now I know
Christmas wishes do come true.

*It's the small things
that make Christmas perfect.*

You deserve all the presents in the world.

I'm in a spin thinking about
sharing this special time with you.

Whatever it takes,
I'll make it back to you for Christmas.

A hug from you is top of my Christmas list.

Have a lovely time,
Not just today and tomorrow,
But for always.

Wherever you are,
You'll always be my Christmas star.

If I could fill a Christmas stocking with hugs,

You would have the fullest one ever.

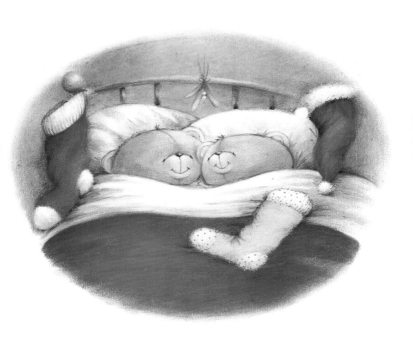

Here's a big Christmas hug in a box
Just for you.

I want to find time this Christmas,

To share a hug or two.

May your Christmas be filled with hug
After hug
After hug.

All I really want for Christmas

Is a special kiss from you.

Christmas is my favourite time of year
Because you'll be here with me.

As I write each Christmas card
And decorate the tree
My thoughts keep turning to you
And how great our day will be.

I'm wishing upon a star
To share the rest of my Christmases with you.

Merry Christmas
To the one I hug...

...and here's to spending
Another wonderful year with you!